CONTENTS

BLUEBIRD POWDER DAY

As the white peaks get closer, my stomach tightens like a knotted rope. I've dreamt of the thrill of my first heli-boarding trip so many times. I've drooled over photos and videos of the rugged mountain range that soars from the ocean to higher than 4,000 metres. I'm face-to-face with the steepest slope I've ever seen. I swallow hard and try to act cool, but my adrenalin levels are way off the charts!

The real deal

I am so excited to be part of this photo shoot on a bluebird powder day! Today's my big chance to prove that I'm the real deal – a pro rider who nails it when the pressure is on.

pro
arder

Community Learning & Libraries
Cymuned Ddysgu a Llyfrgelloedd

This item should be returned or renewed by the
last date stamped below.

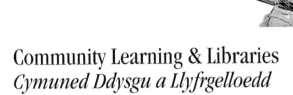
To renew visit:

www.newport.gov.uk/libraries

Cindy Kleh

First published in 2015 by Wayland

Dewey Number: 796.9'39'023-dc23
ISBN: 978 0 7502 9452 2
Library ebook ISBN: 978 0 7502 7398 5

0 9 8 7 6 5 4 3 2 1

Concept by Joyce Bentley

Commissioned by Debbie Foy and Rasha Elsaeed

Produced for Wayland by Calcium
Designer: Paul Myerscough
Editor: Sarah Eason

MIX
Paper from responsible sources
FSC
www.fsc.org   FSC® C104740

Wayland is an imprint of
Hachette Children's Group
Part of Hodder & Stoughton
Carmelite House
50 Victoria Embankment
London EC4Y 0DZ

An Hachette UK Company

www.hachette.co.uk
www.hachettechildrens.co.uk

Printed in China

Acknowledgements: Bomber Industries 16bl; Jeff Brockmeyer 22l, 22c; Dreamstime: Millaus 14l, Monner 2t, 18–19, Francesco Vaninetti 15b; Mark Fox 30l; Getty Images: Johannes Kroemer 28; Paul Krahulec 30-31, 31r; Nora Miller 23; O'Neill 2b, 22r; Shutterstock: Action Photos 26r, Ayazad 11, Brian Finestone 27br, Caleb Foster 9r, Ben Haslam 17tl, Ben Heys 6–7, Blazej Maksym 27l, Ilja Masik 2c, 20–21, 31bl, Mountainpix 3tl, 4–5, 29, Norbert A 8r, Maxim Petrichuk 14r, Samot cover, Strider 27tr, Kaleb Timberlake 8l, Tkemot 3br, Ventura 1, 17br, 24–25, Wildnerdpix 9l; SixSixOne Protection (One Industries, Inc.) 16tr, 17tr.

cover stories

Awesome views

The helicopter touches down and we scramble out with our gear. Suddenly, the wind settles down, and I'm awestruck by the view. Snow covers the landscape like a soft, white blanket. I hold my breath and hop off, landing with a POOF into deep, dry powder. The snow is so deep that it feels like I'm freefalling with every turn as the snow flies in my face. I have to close my mouth to keep from choking on it!

Paid to have fun

Approaching a rocky drop-off, I hear the helicopter's blades thundering near me. I know I'm being filmed, so I head for the highest point, and bust a 360 into bottomless space. I grab my board to keep my body compact as my white and blue world spins around me. White smoke explodes like fireworks going off as I stomp the landing, laughing out loud. I can't believe I'm getting paid to have this much fun!

MAKING IT

Some lucky riders reach their goal of 'going pro.' They are usually passionate about snowboarding and are naturally talented. Pro snowboarders must constantly progress their skills, but they also need a good head for business – snowboarding is a multi-million pound industry as well as an adrenalin sport.

Starting young

Most pro riders start out as 'grommets'. These are young snowboarders who win events at regional snowboarding competitions. By doing so, they bring their skills to the attention of sponsors and filmmakers. They then enter competitions with prize money at stake, and, if successful, are invited to compete in bigger events.

Ticket to ride

Living within a reasonable distance of a mountain resort and buying a season pass are bare necessities to budding professional snowboarders. To make it as a pro, they must spend as many hours of the day as possible making turns and launching off kickers. To fund their dream, some snowboarders teach snowboarding, or take night jobs so that they are free to ride all day.

Riders on film

Some snowboarders are given small parts in snowboard movies. They may then become overnight stars, but that does not happen very often. Snowboarding videos highlight the glory of a professional rider's lifestyle and show them jetting all over the world to enjoy deep powder turns. Few show the hours spent travelling, meeting with the press and sponsors, climbing the pipe over and over to nail a trick, or sitting in a hotel waiting for the weather to clear.

ON THE MAP

A snowboarder kills it on the halfpipe at the X Games in Colorado (left). Steep, deep and rad, Verbier, Switzerland (below), is a favourite destination for photo shoots.

With loads of talent and luck, a professional rider could be invited to compete or film a video anywhere in the world. Here are some of the places to see top riders in action.

Aspen, Colorado

Aspen in Colorado, USA, is host to the X Games. Its dramatic, snow-covered peaks make it one of the best sites in the world. Here, tens of thousands of spectators gather daily during the last weekend of January for a free, up-close view of the world's top winter sport celebrities. Snowboarder X, Skier X, Disabled Skier X, Snowmobile Big Air, slopestyle and superpipe are just some of the sports to see.

Verbier, Switzerland

Home to the Verbier Extremes, Verbier hosts the grandaddy of big-mountain snowboard competitions. Founded in 1996, the Verbier Extremes are held on the Bec des Rosses – a steep, 600-metre sheer face! Today, the contest has grown into an international Freeride World Tour, with four qualifying events around the world and the grand finale at Verbier.

Valdez, Alaska (left), is one of the most remote and challenging snowboarding locations in the world. Banff, Canada (below), has some of the best snowboarding runs in Canada.

Valdez, Alaska

Founded in 1993, the King of the Hill and Queen of the Hill contests put Valdez snowboarding on the map. They are part of the Tailgate Alaska World Freeride Festival, a rider-judged, big-mountain contest. Set on 1,200-plus metres of powder-wrapped vertical, the king and queen of this hill must land huge airs and have nerves of steel. Valdez is also a popular destination for filming snowboard movies because of its endless steep chutes and spectacular, eye-popping scenery.

Banff, Canada

Some professional snowboarders are not cut out for televised contests and all of the hassles of being a snowboarding star. They love their sport but want to stay out of the limelight. These snowboarders often head to Banff, in Canada, which has some of the cleanest snow in the world. Here, pro snowboarders can ride some of the most remote, untouched powder on the planet as their daily job. These boarders choose to be a guide with a helicopter or snowcat tour company. They oversee tours for holiday makers and in their free time shred the Canadian Rockies to the max!

STOKED TO RIDE!

My story by Josh Ort

For my eleventh birthday, my parents booked a series of snowboarding lessons at a local snow dome. The instructor showed us the 'cowboy stance,' the heel and toe edges, and how to traverse down the slope. It was like learning a whole new language! On my first run, the air rushed past my face and shapes of people whooshed by. I saw my parents smiling at the bottom, and I felt so happy! From that second, all I wanted to do was snowboard.

After that, I built up my skills and confidence enough to join the Maverix Snow Camp Youth Development Squad. Joining the squad really helped me to improve my skills. Then, I was lucky enough to be sponsored by Surfanic Clothing – they supplied me with a jacket, snow pants, goggles and gloves for training and competitions.

I trained indoors twice a week at a snow dome near to where I live. This meant that I could ride all year round, then go on holidays to the mountains a couple of times a year. I also practised on a trampoline after school with a training board, doing spins and grabs. Even when I wasn't snowboarding, I still wanted to be active – trying out new moves on my skateboard or practising parkour. I never sat still for long!

I loved learning new tricks and being creative! Plus, the element of danger gave me a sense of achievement when I conquered my fear of doing something. The hardest trick I have ever done is a 720 with a grab – that's two full rotations in the air! It's such a great feeling to land that!

I want to keep improving and perhaps one day compete in the Olympic Games. I'd love to have my own snowboard coaching company so I can teach other kids how to have as much fun as me!

picture posed by model

SNOW SPEAK

Don't get frozen out on the slopes – stoke up on snowboard speak with the Radar guide!

360
a freestyle trick that involves a full-circle rotation

backbowls
bowl-shaped slopes found behind the furthest peaks of a mountain resort

backcountry
off-piste areas that are not within the boundaries of a mountain resort

backside
a trick done with the rider's back facing the pipe wall or slope

banked turns
a snow feature with a nearly vertical slope that causes the rider's body to achieve a horizontal position as he or she carves through the turn

bindings
devices designed to hold a rider's boot to a snowboard

bluebird powder day
a sunny day that follows a big snowstorm

boxes
wide rectangular features, usually made of plastic, that are found in a terrain park

chutes
steep, narrow paths that require tight turns to ride down

cowboy stance
standing on a snowboard with knees bent, legs apart and a tall, relaxed posture

detuned edges
edges of a freestyle board that have been dulled to prevent them catching on boxes and rails

directional board
a freeride board with a wider nose than tail

drop off
the point at which a slope becomes almost vertical

frontside
a trick done with the rider facing the pipe wall or slope

grabs
grabbing the edge of the board while airborne for extra stability and style points

halfpipe/pipe
a U-shaped feature carved out of snow built on a run steep enough to propel the rider into the air

heel/toe edges
the edge of the snowboard closest to the heels/toes of a strapped-in rider

kicker
a large jump that 'kicks' you into the air

parallel GS
a giant slalom race that pits two competitors side by side on identical courses

powder
soft, dry snow that is freshly fallen and a pleasure to ride

quarter pipe
a snow feature with just one wall of a halfpipe

rail jam
a judged competition on a series of rails

regular stance
riding with the left leg in front

rotation
the amount of spinning involved in a trick

Skier X
a boardercross event at the X Games. Disabled Skier X is also held for those riders with physical disabilities

slopestyle
a judged competition held in a terrain park that includes big kickers, rails and other freestyle features

Snowboarder X
a boardercross event featured at the X Games

snow dome
an indoor riding and skiing facility

steeze
displaying class, style and a bit of 'cheese'

stomp
to land a trick solidly

table top jump
a jump designed with a take-off on one end, a flat top and sloped landing on the other

terrain parks
an area within a mountain resort that has freestyle features such as jumps, rails and halfpipes

traverse
to travel down the piste diagonally

tweaking out
stretching out a move to its fullest extension

GLOSSARY

adrenalin
a hormone found in the human body that causes the heart to beat faster and gives a 'rushing' feeling

amplitude
the height that a rider achieves while performing an aerial trick

consecutive
one after the other

Grand Prix
the longest running snowboard competition tour in the USA

incidental contact
elbowing or collisions that happen between competitors that are unintentional

parkour
a method of running over obstacles focusing on efficiency and speed

physical therapy
the medical treatment of someone with a muscular injury or disfunction

podium
a three-tiered structure where riders receive their prizes

prestigious
held in high esteem, very well regarded

sponsors
businesses that support talented riders financially

13

WINNING IT!

A parallel GS (PGS) event features two riders who race simultaneously on identical courses.

Incidental contact is allowed in a boardercross race, but intentional pushing, elbowing or grabbing is not.

Professional riders can choose from several different disciplines within the sport of snowboarding. Few riders can master them all, so for competitions they specialise in the events at which they excel. These are some of the most popular snowboarding events.

Boardercross (BX)

Four to six competitors race in the boardercross event. They compete over a course that can include big kickers, banked turns and bumps. The first rider to cross the finish line wins. Staying ahead of the pack throughout the race helps a rider avoid collisions, especially as incidental contact is allowed during the event. To complete jumps as quickly as possible, BX racers keep their bodies and boards close to the snow.

Giant slalom (GS)

GS is a timed race around gates. To achieve the fastest time, riders explode out of their starting positions and turn above each gate. This reduces skidding and helps the rider gain a direct, quicker line downhill. The closer to the gates riders dare to turn, the faster their times.

Slopestyle and halfpipe

'Slope' and 'pipe' are contests of difficulty, amplitude and 'steeze'. The height and number of rotations of tricks are vital to earning a high score, but 'tweaking out' each move and grab to its fullest will also impress the judges. The more tricks a rider can cram into each run, the better. A rider's final score is the best of two runs.

Competitors try to lay down a solid first run on the halfpipe, then try more difficult tricks on the second to improve their score.

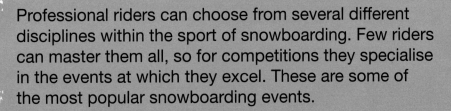

DRESS FOR SUCCESS

Each type of snowboarding competition requires its own equipment, which is specially designed to help a rider win. Riders who are serious about getting on the podium know that the right board, boots, bindings and clothes make a huge difference, and they never compete without a helmet.

boardercross padded sweater

Boardercross (BX)

Most BX riders use a stiff directional board specially designed for BX. Because BX can be very fast and there is contact between riders, they wear a lot of body protection, including padded shorts and sweaters, both equipped with jointed, hard-plastic protectors. A full-face helmet and a mouth guard are used to protect the face and teeth.

Giant Slalom (GS)

GS competitors wear hardboots (similar to ski boots but made especially for snowboarding) and plate bindings – step-in bindings that fit hardboots. They also use a GS alpine board, a narrow, long board with an aggressive side-cut made specifically for powerful, fast turns and stability at high speeds.

hardboot

Slopestyle

Most slope riders wear padded shorts under their trousers. They use a twin-tip board with edges adjusted to not catch on the rail slides.

padded shorts

twin-tip board

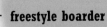

freestyle boarder

Superpipe

To rock the pipe, riders wear lightweight pipe gloves with bright graphics. These emphasise their grabs and make the judges notice them. They ride freestyle boards with sharp edges to carve up the icy walls of halfpipes. Padded shorts under trousers are a good idea for extra protection when learning a new trick.

17

SHAUN WHITE

THE STATS

Name: Shaun White
Date of birth: 3 September 1986
Hometown: Carlsbad, California, USA
Home mountain: Park City, Utah, USA
Job: Professional snowboarder and skateboarder

Sponsored at seven

Before he was a year old, Shaun White had had heart surgery twice. But his heart condition never stopped him from joining in the fun on family skiing holidays. His older brother taught him to snowboard and by the time he was seven, he was offered sponsorship by Burton Snowboards. A couple of years later, he met the skateboarding legend, Tony Hawk, who took him under his wing in the skateboarding world.

Olympic gold

While training for the 2010 Winter Olympics, White perfected his new trick. This was two diagonal rotations with a blind landing (where he couldn't see the landing before his board hit the snow), called The Tomahawk. With help from energy drink manufacturer Red Bull (one of his sponsors) he travelled to his own backcountry training facility by snowmobile or helicopter. These secret training sessions, nicknamed 'Project X', proved to be a success, as Shaun stomped The Tomahawk and won his second consecutive Olympic superpipe gold medal.

Teen X Games star

While White grew in inches and mastered some impressive tricks, he swept five consecutive US national overall snowboarding titles. At the age of 13, he began competing at a professional level and became the first athlete to win four consecutive gold medals at the Winter X Games. He was also first to win gold medals at both Winter and Summer X Games in 2007 and 2011.

Top of the game

White is considered the most recognised and financially successful rider of his generation, with starring roles in multiple video games and snowboarding movies. His career continues to pick up momentum with appearances in TV adverts for his sponsors and a small role in the Hollywood film *Friends with Benefits* (2011). He uses the competitive pressure from other top riders to push himself to constantly progress and learn new tricks.

KILLIN' IT!

Since the invention of snowboarding, records have been made and broken. But there are some that are so amazing, they may stand for decades to come...

Shred 'til you're dead!

Who: Donna Vano
When: Born in 1953
Where: South Lake Tahoe, California, USA
What: Most national snowboarding titles
How: At the age of 40, Donna retired as a pro skier and swapped her skis for a snowboard. She is still competing and winning in GS, slalom, BX, slopestyle and superpipe

Shooting for perfect

Who: Shaun White
When: 18 February 2010
Where: 2010 Winter Olympics, Vancouver, Canada
What: Highest Olympic score in superpipe
How: Perfecting his new trick, The Tomahawk, Shaun scored 48.4 out of 50 on his final superpipe run, winning his second Olympic gold medal

Unbelievable airtime

Who: Mads Jonsson
When: 9 May 2005
Where: Hemsedal, Norway
What: Longest tabletop jump – 57 metres
How: Jonsson performed this feat on a specially built tabletop jump in the backcountry, which took three weeks to build. Its long, steep ramp allowed him to gain the speed he needed without a snowmobile

Split-second speed

Who: Darren Powell
When: 2 May 1999
Where: Les Arcs, France
What: Highest speed on a snowboard – an incredible 201.907 kph
How: Using a specially designed speedsuit and helmet, Powell headed straight down a long, narrow and extremely steep chute

Loads of laps

Who: Tammy McMinn
When: 20 April 1998
Where: Atlin, British Columbia, Canada
What: Most vertical metres snowboarded in 24 hours – 93,124 metres
How: Tammy hired a personal trainer to help her build strength and endurance, and rode an average of seven non-stop hours a day. This helped her to prepare for 24 hours of laps on Paradise Peak, a 2.7432-metre mountain in Idaho's Smoky Mountains, USA

Hucking into space

Who: Terje Håkonsen
When: February 2007
Where: Oslo, Norway
What: Highest air
How: While qualifying for The Arctic Challenge in Oslo 2007, he jumped 9.8 metres off the quarterpipe with a backside 360

Insane riding!

Who: Johan Olofsson (a.k.a. Johan O)
When: 1995
Where: Chugach Range, Alaska, USA
What: Most challenging backcountry line
How: In the movie TB5, Johan O rode a straight line down Cauliflower Chutes (a slope of more than 40 degrees), travelling more than 900 vertical metres in 35 seconds and averaging more than 80 kph.

21

CELIA MILLER

Well established as a snowboarding film star, Celia Miller is now setting her sights on making the US slopestyle team for the 2014 Winter Olympics. Radar asks Celia what it takes to be a pro snowboarder.

How did you get into snowboarding?

When I was 16, my mother told me I needed to get a job, so I started selling lift tickets at my local resort. I made friends with snowboarders and they got me to try it.

Which riders do you admire and why?

I have a ton of respect for the older generation of snowboarders that are still killing it, like Jeremy Jones, Peter Line, Chad Otterstrom, Terje Håkonsen and Janna Meyen-Weatherby. I think many of the younger generation of snowboarders take for granted what is available to them today.

What is your most memorable backcountry filming experience?

Every backcountry trip is an experience whether it's good or bad. I have ridden with some amazing people and had some of the best days snowboarding in my life on those trips. It's a feeling that's hard to describe, so I will keep those moments to myself!

How are backcountry skills and slopestyle skills connected?

Riding the terrain park really helps me with my core tricks. Then, when I take it to the backcountry, I feel confident. I do tend to perfect more new tricks in the backcountry, however. The powder there is a lot softer to land on than terrain parks.

Do you have any strategies or tips for getting on the slopestyle podium?

I pick a run and stick to what I know I can do. It sounds simple, but when I'm in a contest and feeling pressure, it's easy to get intimidated and distracted watching other riders.

What tricks are you currently working on?

Double and triple flips are all the rage. I have been trying a few doubles and rodeos in the backcountry, and I'm working on corking more of my basic tricks. I feel comfortable going upside down, so I am trying to use that to my advantage.

What are the two coolest places you've ever ridden?

Jackson Hole, Wyoming, USA – it's a huge mountain with steep, diverse terrain. And Chamonix, France. This can be a very dangerous place, but the freeriding there is probably some of the best in the world.

THE BACKFLIP

1

2

The aerial backflip is a spectacular and challenging move. Before advancing to a backflip, the rider should be able to perform confident backflips on a trampoline, solid take-offs, grabs and landings on all jumps. He or she should also have mastered 360° rotations.

Why do it?

The backflip is an essential trick for a boarder to master. It is a basic move which, once learned, allows boarders to progress to more advanced moves including many halfpipe tricks. Mastering the backflip not only helps competitors add to their bag of difficult tricks, it also helps a rider learn aerial awareness and safety.

Essential technique

- focus on the lift at take-off
- achieve height to perform rotation
- pinpoint landing site at highest point of the jump

HOW IT'S DONE

1. The rider chooses a medium-size jump, and focuses on gaining lift at the take-off point.
2. He then brings his knees towards his body and curls into a tight ball of rotating energy.
3. Once the rider has rotated 90°, he looks back for his landing point.
4. The rider lands with his weight centred over the board. He then bends his knees to absorb the impact on landing.

3

4

NAILIN' THE RAILS

Just as skateboarders 'slide' on rails, snowboarders perform similar moves . Here are some of the tricks seen at rail competitions, known as 'rail jams'.

Gap rail

A gap in a rail makes it necessary for a rider to jump from one section to the other, making the move more challenging and daring. Some gap rails have a gap between the take-off (jump onto the rails) and the rail.

Rainbow rail

These rails are shaped in a curve like that of a rainbow (hence their name). The first rainbow rails that snowboarders tried to slide were young trees that had bowed over in the woods. Now, rainbow rails can be found in terrain parks in different heights, widths and variations.

Kinked rail

Kinked rails and boxes have a 'flat-down-flat' section. This is a horizontal platform followed by an incline and another flat section. Some kinked rails have several flat-down-flat sections in a row.

Frontside boardslide

During a boardslide, the snowboarder slides at an angle perpendicular to the rail. The term 'frontside' was first used in surfing to describe a move that was carried out facing the wave. In the case of freestyle snowboarding, it means that the rider is facing uphill *towards* the slope or halfpipe wall.

This rider is jumping from one side of a gap rail, and landing in a frontside boardslide down the other side — a difficult trick, if he makes it!

This move is achieved by bending the knees to hug the arch of the rainbow rail, while riding with the board pointing towards the end of the rail.

This rider is boarding on a kinked rail, and is preparing to slide into the dip of the flat-down-flat.

A frontside boardslide is performed on the tail of the board. It is important to stay centred and avoid catching the edge of the board on the rail.

BOARDING TO WIN

After the invention of the first 'modern' snowboard in the late-1970s, riders started to compete against each other to be the fastest, highest boarder. As equipment improved, moves were pushed to the limit and competitions became big crowd-pullers.

Suicide Six

The first National Snowboard Championships took place at Suicide Six, a small ski resort in Vermont, USA, in 1982. The event consisted of a steep, downhill race, and some racers were timed at more than 96 kph. The contest evolved into the US Open Snowboard Championships – now one of the sport's most prestigious events, with prizes totalling US$250,000.

The halfpipe is born

In 1983, Tom Sims organised the first halfpipe contest at Soda Springs Ski Bowl near Lake Tahoe, California, USA, on the world's first man-made pipe. In 1985, Breckenridge Resort in Colorado, USA, built a pipe with five-foot walls for the Snowboarding World Championships. After the contest, the pipe became a permanent feature at the resort on which riders could practise. By 1988, every major resort was scrambling to make its own pipe. During the early-1990s, the snowboarding craze had swept Europe, and European countries began hosting world championships.

Jake Burton was one of the first snowboarders to take to the slopes. The skier-turned-snowboarder is also the founder of Burton Snowboards, a leading American snowboard manufacturer.

X Games rock!

The first Winter X Games were held in 1997 at Big Bear Lake, California, USA. The event was aired on TV, giving many people their first real taste of extreme snowboarding. In 2002, the Games moved to Aspen, Colorado, where they have remained. In 2008, X Games XII saw a 33 per cent increase in TV viewers from the year before, and the International Olympic Committee (IOC) began looking at X Games events to add to the Olympic line up, such as slopestyle.

Parallel giant slalom (PGS) has been an Olympic sport since snowboarding was first featured at the 1998 Winter Olympics.

Olympic glory

Snowboarding first appeared at the 1998 Winter Olympics in Nagano, Japan. Superpipe and parallel giant slalom (PGS) became events in 2002, and snowboard cross was added to the list at the 2006 Games. With snowboarding's proven record for grabbing the attention of youth viewing and selling TV advertising space, a further event, slopestyle, has been added to the 2014 Olympics in Sochi, Russia.

RADAR SPENDS A WEEK WITH BOARDERCROSS SPECIALIST, KIM KRAHULEC, AS SHE PREPARES FOR THE CHEVY GRAND PRIX COMPETITION

KIM KRAHULEC

blog   **news**   **events**

SUNDAY

I rode the boardercross course at Copper Mountain, Colorado, today, really working on my starts. I finally nailed some good ones. My gym workout was light today – I did two hours of weight-training with some stretching. My knee's been swollen so I'm hoping that it will heal in time for the Grand Prix later this week.

MONDAY

I tuned and waxed my boards, and packed my bag for Boreal, California. I went to physical therapy because my knee is still swollen and aching.

TUESDAY

I got up at 4am to make my 7am flight to Reno, Nevada, USA. I slept in the team van all the way up to Boreal Mountain Resort. The house we are staying in is sweet! I went to the hill to register and check out the course.

blog   news   events

WEDNESDAY

I slept until 8am. I inspected the course in detail and took a couple of training runs. My knee really ached, and it kept me from riding my best. It was so frustrating! I wrapped it in ice after I trained — hoping that would help it heal before the big event tomorrow.

THURSDAY

Race day. My knee still really hurts, but I decided to race regardless. I had to fight through the semi-final heat, but I made it to the finals! The final heat was a tough one. I had a bad start and got tangled up with one of my closest friends. I was still able to somehow take third place and win US$3,000 — not bad for a day of riding! We packed up the van right after the race and headed home. It had been a long day and I was tired.

FRIDAY

We finally arrived back home at 2am. I was so tired, all I wanted to do was sleep and I collapsed into bed!

SATURDAY

Our coach seemed to have no sympathy for us! We spent three hours working sooo hard in the gym today, and then I headed to physical therapy to check out my knee again. It's been a crazy week, but nailing that tough boardercross course and winning solid cash to pay my bills has made it all worthwhile!

SNOW'S UP!

Snowboarding is fast and fun,
so get to the slopes and drop in!

People to talk to

British Snowboard Association
The BSA manages local, regional and
national competitions and hosts the
annual FIS World Cup Big Air:
www.snowboardclub.co.uk/bsa

**Tamworth and
High Wycombe SnowDomes**
Check out two of the biggest
snow domes in the UK at:
www.snowdome.co.uk
www.wycombesummit.co.uk

**American Association of Snowboard
Instructors (AASI)**
For all sorts of information visit:
www.aasi.org

Reads, DVDs & Apps

Be amazed by these snowboarding films:
That's It, That's All (Quiksilver, 2008)
Catch the Vapors (Standard Films, 2007)

Top snowboarding titles include:
Extreme Halfpipe Snowboarding Moves
by Mary Firestone (Capstone, 2003)

Snowboarding (To the Limit)
by Paul Mason (Wayland, 2008)

Download the *snowEdge* app to judge
your speed, elevation and airtime. Take a
look at *iTrailMap* for high-resolution trail
maps of your favourite snowboard resorts:
www.itunes.com
https://market.android.com

INDEX